The Year of the Rabbit

POETRY

To Lin & Annalise,

with so much love

from Kozi & 'the Rabbit!

3/29/2012

The Year
of the
Rabbit

POETRY

KOZI NASI

iUniverse, Inc.
Bloomington

The Year of the Rabbit
Poetry

iUniverse books may be ordered through booksellers or by contacting:

iUniverse
1663 Liberty Drive
Bloomington, IN 47403
www.iuniverse.com
1-800-Authors (1-800-288-4677)

ISBN: 978-1-4759-3578-3 (sc)
ISBN: 978-1-4759-3579-0 (ebk)

Library of Congress Control Number: 2012912081

Printed in the United States of America

iUniverse rev. date: 07/10/2012

To Lover . . .

A Poet State of Mind

For poet was not my intention
till you came along
bearing his name
wind . . . wasn't it?
Ah, the lucky coincidences!

As I drink and spill my troubles
in tight verses and loose rhymes,
poet is still not my intention
at all;
it has always been,
in fact,
my most insanely sane state of mind!

From

From a little faraway land I come . . .
within this planet, yet from a very different world,
a world of heroic legends and sacrificing fairies,
a world of bestowed honor and banished voodoos
where a human can never reach the sky
and the doubts of subconsciousness roam the cold dark grounds
where imagination rules and fantasy is fierce,
where the sky hangs low and the stars burn faster,
where birds sing loud and waves of blue waters splash angrily on
rocky shores,
where scents of beautiful women are stolen by naked flowers
and the rages of jealous men are enthused by wild animals . . .

The Creation

And so the Master created me:
the perfect nature's malformation,
the beautiful face
covered carelessly by dark-brown curls,
the olive eyes defined by the long, arched brows,
the soft nose above the juicy red lips,
the delicate long neck leading the way south
as the stubborn breasts look up through their nipple eyes.

Pleased with HIS creation, in a glass box HE put me,
and ever so proudly HE showed me around.
A match I had become,
HIS imperfections' perfect match,
I had become!
And painfully HE loved me.
To comfort HIS lost soul to HIS slow death
HE kept me around . . .

Woman

I try and I try,
every waking hour, I try,
as I have been for the past
thirty-seven years and ten months, give or take.

I dig and I dig,
constantly deep down, I dig,
yet empty handed I seem to return,
never exactly finding that for which I yearn . . .

I think and I think,
good and bad thoughts altogether, I think,
gladly walking to my dying hole,
as it is my own thoughts that in the end will kill me . . .

I cry and I cry,
warm, salty tears, I cry
quietly by myself, when no one can see me.
my cheeks' favorite waterfalls they are . . .

I talk and I talk
honestly, clearly, eloquently, I talk,
and brutal I sound every time
I open my big, beautiful mouth . . .

I laugh and I laugh
loud, wholeheartedly, I laugh
until I feel my lungs scream
for pure oxygen to inhale . . .

I sing and I sing
soft, sweet melodies, I sing
lullabies, operettas, even a little cabaret
à la late '20s decadent Berlin . . .

I kiss and I kiss
passionately, slowly, and tenderly I kiss,
eyes closed, at times open as well
so I can see the pleasure I give and receive . . .

I love and I love,
oh, so madly, fully, completely, I love.
I dive head first in its magic ocean
and I drink it all, to the very last drop . . .

I live and I live,
every day I live,
not as if it were my last,
as if it were my very first, instead,
tirelessly chasing satisfaction,
fearlessly pushing away useless regret.
Most days I stubbornly win,
others, I proudly fail . . .

And by the way,
I am woman.
Have we met?

The Battle and the War

I am a pacifist.
I do not choose wars.
They definitely choose me.

I carefully pick my battles,
all the little battles
within the big war,

And that's how every time I win:
by only half the time
choosing me.

I

I came out happy and in peace,
a love child, I am told,
a beautiful, curly haired blonde
who talked early and couldn't wait to walk.

I was,
I used to be,
I was brought up to be,
I wanted to be,
I was told to be,
I grew to be,
I became,
I turned into,
I am,
I try to be,
I dream to be,
still . . .

I used to be a good kid.
I then turned into a good woman.
I am, as of now,
an imperfectly content being.
Perfection I grew tired of chasing!

I vow to remain
a most tormented,
colorfully unraveling,
desirable human
at my own very best!
Can you love me like that?

Saved!

(un-brainwashed)

If these walls could talk,
they'd tell you . . .
that I was born here
with a miserable famous name
to barely separate me
from all the identical sad clowns.
Fooled they had me from birth
and before me,
my butterfly mother
and the dying soldier father.

If these walls could talk,
they'd tell you . . .
I was lobotomized before they sent me home
claiming a birth defect.
Relieved they had me of my thinking part
and kept it in an ugly jar
to wash it and later give it back, no doubt!
Blaming it all on the red dust
that fell every early afternoon
atop my balcony without a view . . .
Accidentally, they forgot to put it back,
so I matched the other zombies
for twenty-one years . . .

If these walls could talk,
they'd tell you . . .
I grew up here
lonely,
alone,
roaming aimlessly, a misfit,
free, with no places to go,
loved, with no heart to bleed,
missed, with no soul crying for me,
the empty cranium calling in vain,
the forgotten part in the ugly jar.

If these walls could talk,
they'd tell you . . .
I didn't tear when I left.
I didn't even turn my head,
see, only because I didn't know
it could actually hurt,
one day very soon,
it could really hurt that bad,
the day when I would return
to get back what they stole from me at birth
only to find the precious jar
waiting for me
in rubbles of dirt
and piles of depressed time,
forgotten,
unopened,
unbroken,
untouched!

If these walls could talk,
they'd tell you . . .
I come back here from time to time,
sit alone by this painful gray rock,
and swallow
a plate of dirt with a bottle of rain
to remember the story of the saved brain in the jar
that miraculously they forgot to wash out!
And think
of how it would be
the day I came to finally stay,
the day my ashes would be scattered here
in my beloved winding olive road
that always leads me to the deep blue sea
that forever will love me so . . .

If these walls could talk,
they'd tell you . . .
there's no museum for me.

The Impaired Generous

(the only life I gave away)

I've been giving all my life
everything to everyone.
Haters, I gave them love.
Lovers, I gave them lust—
asking for anything back
was never my style,
but in a last sad spring
when . . .
in a metal room with one-too-many locks and keys,
like the trembling little canary,
fearful, I flew through,
strange voices ushered me in.
Cold hands made my bed,
hard brushes combed away my skull,
strong winds unclothed me,
cruelly freezing my feathery wings.
Unwillingly, I breathed in the suffocating clouds,
counting backward five, four, three . . .

Swallowed captive by the tired ether,
watching from above the cold hands butchering me—
one by one they scraped away
all layers of my flesh,
dissecting me
like the lifeless frog
in a dragging class of premed physiology,
gutting me empty
like the mouth of a grave . . .
Inside the hungry womb a fainting candle I lit
to mark the silent wake
before the tearless funeral.
The pale flame echoed through my body,
unable to burn me whole,
my ashes annoyed
they'd have to wait some more . . .

Days later I came to . . .
lifeless,
weak,
on the gray metal tray,
counting backward ten, nine, eight . . .
bloodless,
unburied,
barely breathing, left for barely dead!

No God could ever put me back together,
no God could ever forget,
much like the living
can never be reclaimed by the passed!
For giving
I can no longer take!

KOZI NASI

Stranger Needed

Alone, I am tonight
listening to the tunes of a dead woman,
pleasuring my fleeting memory cells
with the echo of an eternal jazz sound,
button-pushing my own melancholy
as I slowly swallow
sober, unsalted tears.

Every note attempts to distract me
with stories I know,
stories I've lived,
stories I've made up,
stories I've written about
my stories . . .

But I know all of them,
was there for every single one,
ever since I dug my well
and stuffed it with
one story after another,
one very late night at a time . . .

Yet my melancholy
takes the best of me
and I crave the stories of a stranger.

Tonight,
not just any stranger will do.
Tonight,
I need the one with the sad tea and the burnt cigarettes
to throw me a bone,
hell,
to throw me
the whole closet full of skeletons!

And quiet as a little mouse,
I shall listen . . .

Reborn!

Happy people went to that place of Holy
to borrow some flame.
The priest, ever so happy to comply,
will give it to them all with a smile.
The flame will come home,
will burn some more,
till midnight and beyond . . .

The happy people will obliviously celebrate
the rebirth of the Lord's only Son
as if they are freshly reborn themselves!

Little do those happy people know
that they took away from my time,
from my happy moment,
from my one-of-a-kind, limited-edition biblical moment
of a naive attempt at my own rebirth!

Surrounded by happy people,
I generously pass around my smile
like the Holy Flame
that burns patiently to rebirth both Jesus and me.

Until all lipstick was wiped and forgotten
at each of the five deep lines
at the two corners of two good eyes,
I waited to be born again, much like Jesus,
but . . . perhaps next time . . .

Hop-hop said the blue bunny,
Happy Rebirth, unfazed little people!

As

Timid
as the first electrifying kiss she did not get from a boy,
Tender
as the very first touch that made her feel all grown up,
Pleasured
as the underskin tangled in the shivering flesh,
Flawless
as the melody she sang that spring night after two cigarettes,
Moist
as the four teary eyes at the moment of the tumultuous good-bye,
Clear
as the first red dawn alone,
Breathless
as the color-blind, joyous air surrounding the happy rainbow,
Complete
as the only time she was truly found,
Calm
as the day of the big surrender,
Fragile
as the last prophetic farewell!

Picture Frames

Memories . . .
I hang them on my cold, colorless walls
like empty, expensive picture frames
in a failed attempt to decorate
the see-through canvas
I'm not allowed to paint.

Slowly I've built my own collection
of countless memories I'd rather not forget—
places,
faces,
lovers,
friends,
past,
present,
all the same!

This midnight
I redecorate,
switch around empty frames.
Like my children, I love them all.
Like my undead lovers, I remember them . . .

Yet I can't take anyone out
and it seems there's no room to add new ones . . .

Whom I love, I can't choose—
only whom I keep
is still up to me!

Another Rushed Decision

Through a flesh-felt sigh and a breathless moan,
I lost my religion last night
(too impure to keep up with it!)—
you know, the one where
I don't show up for my own confessions!

For I am the nun
and the priest in one,
thus,
no mercy
no mercy
no mercy for me!

Infatuation

(while we wait . . .)

I could've sworn I met you in another life,
in a life where time stood still
and we made love endlessly
and pitied the world going by.
But we have yet to meet, haven't we?

And the world I'm in now
is just too small for me
to fit all my lovers in.
Thus I will save this life as is,
and in the next one,
you shall taste the sinner in me.
But we have yet to meet, haven't we?

And in the meantime,
we shall continue to exist
through sadly implied verse
and poorly selected melody.
But we have yet to meet, haven't we?

In a parallel universe,
you and I are two of a kind,
saved for each other on purpose,
sitting comfortably in the ninth cloud,
you,
making me jealous of your exes,
me,
seducing you with my smile,
and we stare at each other's eyes,
like that,
wrinkled of time . . .
yet the crazy fire burning feverishly inside.
None of us get tired.
We can do this all night,
until the sheets are ripped
and the bed is torn apart,
that big old rusty box
that has been there
for every single scream and sigh . . .
But we have yet to meet, haven't we?

Someone told me a long time ago
they would savor me
as a timeless "could have been" love story
to share with their grandkids.
Pathetic, I thought at the time
(not knowing he'd keep his promise),
as I blew the last good-bye kiss!
I don't want this to happen to us.
The world must end then . . .
not the one I now breathe in, but
that yet-to-exist one, with us in it . . .
But we have yet to meet,
haven't we?

The Man and the Little Girl.

For the only man I've ever known
who got to realize the little girl
who still exists inside of me . . .

For the child I've always known
who still lives inside the woman in me
who only one man really got to see . . .

For you, my one and only,
for you, my thee,
you may have them both!
The woman and the little girl,
love you the same
truly . . . deeply . . . dearly!

On!

Hello, old soul.
I will come
over tonight.
I will let you in,
if you wish.
We've finally reached
that happy place!

Let's whisper,
again and again and again,
sweet nothings
as you sweat,
and I
heavy breathe . . . ah!

Hello, old soul.
Old habits die hard, they say,
yet yours never did,
and mine,
still whispering, shh shh shh shh!
It's your fault, you know—
me,
sinfully guilty,
you,
always happy to please!

Let's whisper, old soul,
again and forever,
sweet nothings
as you
shamelessly sweat
and I
deliriously breathe . . . ah!

Whisper with me, old soul,
whisper away,
all the way in!

The (missing) Tattoo

There's a little red-eyed frog tattoo
at the lowest of my back.
It reminds me of that night you converted
into the prince you never wanted to be
and that deep down you've regretted ever since
(still blaming the magic kiss I forgot
on the tip of your tongue).

There's a little red-eyed river frog tattoo
that I always longed to get
but never did.
It reminded me of your need to remain
the eternal leaping frog,
jumping back and forth
to and fro me . . .

True

I cover my face with a colorful butterfly mask
so the world won't see the dragon sleeping inside.
I cover my eyes with big dark glasses
so the world won't see the fire exhaling from my eyes.
I cover my lips with the deepest shade of red
so the world won't see the bloodstains from dinner last night.
I cover my body with the longest Jesuit priest's cloak
so the world won't see the shameful perfection of my lines.
I cover my feet with the highest feathery heels
so the world won't see the disappearing act every night I pull
to come find you . . .

And I do!

I unmask at your door and let out a moan or two,
remove my glasses and set the fiery eyes free,
wipe off my lips and lick them moist,
disrobe and let my soft skin breathe deep,
bare my feet and run to you . . .

And I do!

As in the day I was born,
happy,
naked,
screaming,
perfectly imperfect,
natural
as the terrifying wilderness of the jungle,
I give myself to you . . .

And I do!

The fiery-eyed, bloody-lipped, eager dragon in me
performs wild, crazy dances for you tonight—
no choreography, no taught steps,
no rules of law, not even laws of nature,
no masks or covers, no artificial layers apply—
my one-and-only melody of the flesh loud can be heard
with the sounds of the burning lust
from the superficially hypocritical world.
Freed at last, you and I,
just you
and
just I!

You

The distance between us,
much like the time between us,
stretches through
worlds
and dawns
and sunrises
and horizons
and sunsets
and dusks
and eager dawns again . . .

To hurry you, I do not wish,
but only because it feels
it's just not meant to be . . .

All odds are against us,
all gods as well.
Olympus got awoken
by the sighs of our flesh.
Jealous got those pesky gods
even angry, I could tell.
Much more than them humans,
we've managed to upset them all!

But what about you and me lover,
will we ever meet again?
I promise, I'll do whatever you wish.
Yes, I know you'll try whatever I ask.
I shall give up all my guilty pleasures,
all but one, I swear.
I shall give up my tears,
the clothes that hurt me,
and my high heels too . . .
shall give them all to your *eppur si muove*
in a last attempt to bribe your muse,
to get her to fly up to Mount Olympus
to bring me back my Aphrodite.
Venus, Hades, and Zeus all mighty
to ugly me pretty,
to shy me uninhibited,
to sacrifice me softly
with that friendly pain divine . . .
And prep me for you,
you handsome, tall, beautiful you!

And when my eyes are wet again,
my mouth moist,
my breathing noisy,
my skin abloom,
when my luscious curls
have grown to cover
the two teardrops of flesh,
perhaps then
the gods will feel ready
to allow me
to meet you
again,
all over again,
you . . . you . . . you!

A Funny Game of Love and Hate

You've hated the strut of my walk from the first time you noticed me.
You've hated the sound of my voice from the first moment you heard it.
You've hated the sparkle of my eyes from the first time you gazed at me.
You've hated the waves of my hair from the first time you watched the wind play with it.
You've hated the taste of my mouth from the first time you savored it.
You've hated the stretch of my neck from the first time you bent it.
You've hated the softness of my skin from the first time your fingers fluttered against it.
You've hated the warmth of my breasts from the first time you rested on them.
You've hated the cinch of my waist from the first time you danced me.
You've hated the arch of my back from the first time you leaned on it.
You've hated that deep oasis where I deliriously glow from the first time you drank in it.
You've hated me naked from the first time you made love to me that spring of many moons ago.
You've hated the smell of my flesh from the first time I rolled under your nose.
You've hated my shadow from the first time you watched me leave.
But that's why you love me!
. . .

I hate the idea that you exist not constantly next to me.
I hate the school girl crush you've inflicted on me since ninety-three.
I hate how my blood evaporates from my head when I see you.
I hate how all layers of my skin shiver when I think of you.
I hate how I ache when you're not here to touch me.
I hate how I crumble every time you kiss me.
I hate how I crave you to take me completely.
I hate how I yearn for you to ignite me and burn me.
I hate how you manage to forget yourself with me.
I hate how unbelievably you still want me.
I hate how you read me like your favorite book.
But that's why I love you!

Beyond the Wooden Bridge

There is a little wooden bridge
beyond the point of pleasure
that awaits me to cross it,
where the winding olive road
that ends at the deep green sea
draws me to follow it . . .

Ever the blind goddess,
I go by scent alone.
The murmuring sigh of the rocky shore
lingers in my pierced ears
and gently guides me to destiny . . .

The address is simple:
Second universe,
Seventh sky,
Cloud nine!

I make it there barefoot,
a silkiest veil but covers my flesh,
white butterflies fold the dark waves of my hair
in a messy row or two,
the good eyes are the jewels
in exchange for the toll
of the olive road and the deep green sea
for eyes—
I shall not need them anymore . . .

At the very end
of the airy hall,
I check in at room Cerebral,
with its single red door and no key.
A handsome dark angel lets me in.
A lonely iron bed decorates it.
No walls surround it.

I take one last deep breath
and fill my mouth with pure blood
only to spit it seconds later
in the dark angel's heart.
Wings ready, he flies away,
thanking me
for the *bloody Kozi!*

In the old bed I quietly climb.
The white butterflies off my hair go loose—
curled up in fetal position,
I wait
and wait
for you . . .

At Infinity Hotel
in the single spacious bed
in the keyless, wall-less room,
until my dying breath,
I wait and wait for you,
for eternity that begins
beyond the wooden bridge!

KOZI NASI

Dreamers

Dreamers are you and I, lover,
pathologically euphoric dreamers we are.
Certified by the very long time together,
attested by the way we've lived our lives.

Your very first dream you shared with me
and it spun my world around.
As fate would have it, it happened to be mine as well,
so we both mistook it for the divine sign
that together we must stay.

My very first dream I shared with you,
it brought a tear to your eye
and you promised we'd soon go back to that
and visit it one little verse at a time—
you promised, not I . . .

Dreamers are you and I, lover,
fatalistic, delusional dreamers we are
that decided deliriously, like in the best dream,
to run away and trick life
and forever foolishly hide.

So hiding in our dream house, we've lived since
for roof, our bubble of lust,
for walls, our arms intertwined,
for floor, our tangled toes,
for windows, our sparkling eyes,
for light, our beating hearts . . .

We still live there, you and I,
drawers full of shelved dreams we never bother to visit,
most shared, some not,
even those we don't mind.
By now, you have the years for patience.
By now, I no longer have the time.

Dreamers are you and I, lover,
melodramatic, eternal dreamers, we are
drunk in fortune-teller's potions of love,
crushed by stars,
lifted by clouds,
exhausted by fairy tales of pseudo-charmed lives,
made lazy by choice,
woken up each day by desire,
abandoned by time . . .

We shall die dreamers, you and I, lover.
It's the heroic pact we made many moons passed,
happy to have cheated life in our own terms,
misdiagnosed, mindless dreamers,
in a universe of our own
that this world never got!

Prelude

Each weekday belongs to him,
each weekend, to the other,
me and MY crazy
me and MY lover.

I lost track.
I lost count.
Visitations are hard.
Pleasing them both
(it's always)
the easy part!

Gemini

It dawned on me suddenly
on a warm May night
I've been sharing my bed
with two men at once
and back and forth I switch
in my most perfect Gemini ...

Lover sleeps peacefully right by my side,
his head on my breasts
(his favorite pillow),
his arms like tree branches
hugging my waist.
In between my thighs
his magic hands rest.

And me,
I stay awake, this wet May night,
me and my thoughts
trying to remember how it all began,
this enchanted story
of my most perfect Gemini ...

It started the very usual way,
on a brand-new January
and the first of the alphabet
in that faraway land forsaken of all fairies ...

KOZI NASI

Out of the blue there came
this one mysterious ingénue
who unknowingly ignited a crazy new beginning
by abruptly ending
the one merely existing.

In a game of cards
a beautiful fortune-teller
his future read him right out loud.
While passionately kissing him one last time,
she gave him six months to live
and wished him all the good luck!
(Ever the eternal optimist,
he took it all in stride,
eagerly hunting for fresh new life,
spears a-blazing,
prey aplenty,
never too many!)
Until
fate helped him straight to my door,
a gray one on the first floor,
marked with the numbers 121.

Magic happened in that little room.
They wrote songs about it later on,
names they called it with envy
in that young forsaken town.

I still hear the hurrying steps,
the stumping shoes approaching fast
carrying potions of lust and sex
for us to take and to forget
the game of cards
and the luscious fortune-teller's sighs!

Now
a long time has gone by,
life and time again,
only for me to realize
I've been sharing my bed
for the longest ever
at once, with these two men:
the angel sleeping peacefully next to me
and the devil on my back
torturing me within,
the most legendary threesome,
with me always in the middle.

And I've come to like them both,
angel lover and dreamy devil.
I crave them both.
I yearn for the two
as I was fatally reminded
with a poisoned adrenaline shot
at this place from *Moby Dick*
where I tipped sixty-nine pennies
and tore up the cup with my bloody red lips
from which I drank my thirst
and his utter loss for words . . .

Next time I see you
I shall keep you to myself,
the wind sighed softly on that breezy night
with my head on his chest,
a warm tear in my eye,
and longing to belong,
Yes, please, said I . . .

Like the desperate, empty ashtray,
I need the devil's cigarette breath,
the smoky clouds shaped like Ps
out of his lips, exhaled my way.

Now they both lie next to me,
both rest on each one of my breasts,
equally feeding off my heartbeats,
equally pulling me their selfish way.

It took me awhile to realize
with these two men I've shared my bed,
I've gulped happily their shivering breaths
to such eternal free fall,
unconditionally surrendering myself.

Yes,
angel lover and dreamy devil both get to stay
in my warm, wide bed,
for in lover
I have found
my most suitable Gemini!

On Your Birthday

This is not a fantasy.
People cannot pay money for this.
It is the tale of two lovers
as opposite as they could be,
bound together by lust and passion.

I never had the exact shade of green
for mine to be your dreamt-of eyes,
was never as tall
or head to toe a natural blonde.
Yet here I am, naked as the sky,
standing closest on your left arm,
wondering if today's birthday
will be the "one-too-many" enough—
no doubt, me
the sometimes-guilty
no doubt, you
the sometimes not-so-pure one.

I get tired of you sometimes,
you probably more tired of me,
for a tiring compromise it is.

I still watch you when you sleep,
still trying not to miss
a single one of your heart's beats,
in awe of how you're still here.
The packed luggage never left my sight.
You love me for my imperfections.
You can never love me more than Greatness—
her you must go get,
beyond that glorious valley of my lowest back
that forever shall bear your golden name.

Though my spirit wanders
like a fragile little bird,
I always return.
I always come back,
trembling gently in your restless hands,
and I'd gladly die a thousand deaths
just to give you what you need,
to let you take all that you wish!

Perhaps with you I will grow old,
perhaps with you I will get to be
sixty-nine, ninety-six,
even more, why not?
You are saved your place in Heaven,
but not me, I'm afraid—
I cannot join you up there.
Someone else holds my ticket
to the darkest Purgatory
as he smiles and waves at me in the ninth fiery ring.
I should have your permission by then
since I'm the one that loves you best!

Another birthday is here . . .
with just you,
with just me.
All I can do is hope you're happy
and satisfied
and fulfilled
and remembering
that once,
many birthdays ago,
I was the one thing
you wanted most!

Heaven can wait!

An old-fashioned glass holds my drink tonight,
the smoothest Grey Goose floats the ice
with a thick lemon twist
to enhance the flavor and scent.
Heaven can wait, it can still wait . . .

(Lover's off to Greatness
though he still owes me
a strawberry ball
at only sixty-nine pennies.)

That is not the sound of the waves
corroding the forgiving shore
a little more
each time they tease it
a little more,
each time they feed it
their salty, bubbly foam
with a hard, cold splash.

It's the sound of the flesh instead,
at first quiet and gentle
and then loudest when mad.
Heaven can wait, it can still wait . . .

Am I getting old for you, love,
or younger by the day?
You must pick one, my angel,
choose what you want—
there's only so many parts
for you I could play.
Heaven can wait, it can still wait . . .

Went to the moon and back
looking for the answer
to the everlasting question:
Am I here for you,
or are you here for Greatness?
I never got the answer.
I'm good at many things
but never that perfect.
How much time is there left?
Heaven can wait, it can still wait . . .

KOZI NASI

As the restless camel, I quench my thirst
in your liquid love's oasis.
Happily I float in it
like the ice cubes in my old-fashioned.
Willingly I release you
into your desirable Greatness.
(Did I even stand a chance?)
That will be your ever-wondering answer,
while I still hold on
for dear, sweet death
to my irreconcilable regrets!

You wink at me, irresistible,
with your blood-craving eyes.
It is the season of feeding—
vampires are all out!
But Heaven can wait,
it will have to wait . . .

Dance Me!

To tiptoe all over your heart was not my intention,
yet I dance and dance, delirious
and oblivious of the trouble I have caused
now that the damage is done . . .

You bend me
and spin me,
lift me up in the air,
throw me around,
catch me so I don't fall
when I bother get down
from the angel that holds me,
from the devil that teases
with Pandora's black box,
clueless that she loves me too,
enough to trust me with the secret code
to steal the box open
and give devil the last hard blow.

On my way to you, I wish to weep.
In the sunset room you wait comfortably.
Slowly, I approach to join you,
a glass of wine in one hand for me,
a snifter of cognac for you in the other.
The happy flesh forgets to breathe.
Unclothed, as in the day I was born,
I ask you softly if you mind my dancing.
With the evil smile you shake your head no,
grab the wine from my hand,
wiping my lower lip with yours.
Squeezed in the warmest embrace,
you dance me, dance me to the end,
eyes locked,
bodies not wanting to behave . . .

With every sunset our dance begins,
it ends with every sunrise.
I love you not because I need you,
I love you because I love to love!

S.P.E.A.K!

Raspy,
like the scratchy sound
of the forgotten jazz singer
in a smoked-up cabaret,
my voice sounds tonight.
The vocal cords are missing.
I finally shipped them off to you.
I couldn't suffer anymore
through your persistently begging requests
for my sweet, slow melody,
the one that shoots me to Heaven,
the one that always takes you
to that hazy place of delirium!

The wind shall be delivering
the timbre of my voice to you,
and with its lightest breeze
I shall beg you to
s.p.e.a.k.
exactly the way
I always invite you
to ever
so
gently
slide in!

Pitchy,
like the off-key sound
of the missing string
on the old acoustic guitar,
my song sounds tonight.
Demure is my mood,
just like this old cabaret
that we've called the Abby
with its secret-covered walls
and long purple curtains
that reek of the best Cubans!

I know you're listening—
how could you not?
Oblivious of its echo,
I sang that song for you.
It's your melody now,
and I forever shall call it
your symphony!

So come closer, over here,
do me one big favor
and gently as ever
in your smoothest,
raspiest
voice,
only
just
s.p.e.a.k!

A Bedtime Story

Aged is the wine that slowly finds its way down my throat,
from a rare vine, the excited sommelier explains.
The crystal glass is round and heavy,
my kind is he,
from a civilization recently declared extinct.

The bed is an old fallen tree in the middle of the forest
with long, tall branches for posts, where he ties me sometimes—
a restless Kama Sutra to be called waits in vain.

Dark are the sheets on my pale skin.
Like a jealous young lover they wrap around me tight,
for a jealous man he is.
The magic fingers lift me up to cloud nine,
the snakelike tongue slithers along the flesh between my ribs,
the bloody lips give birth to fireflies,
the wettest kiss to the burning sin delivers me,
arched,
bent,
stretched,
pulled,
pushed,
again and again,
sighs,
moans,
groans—

the a cappella song of my flesh
lit up by the fierce lightning
of such postpubescent rain dance,
charged by the very vocal thunder,
erupted by the impatient volcano,
parched for its liquid, melting heat,
he goes long
I crave deep . . . ah!

Covered in sparkles of Venus's sweat,
I tremble and shake
as the rings of my Saturn squeeze
every single drop of his Jupiter
until the forest to lust gives in completely
and the wilderness loses its rejuvenating sleep!

The water flows calmly from a spring nearby
and these lines,
these lines are tonight's bedtime story,
the very grown-up kind . . .

Cleopatra

The longest sandy desert
I walked for you, sweet lover,
the driest burning dunes
I camel crossed for you,
so badly I desired that one desert rose
that Cleopatra has hidden deep in the twisted Nile
for you
to wander through time,
and me,
to want to find it back,
desperately, for you!

I envision it in my head, you know—
all the red-hot purple petals
of that sweet, luscious desert rose,
desired and wanted,
touched and captured,
seeded and planted,
watered and pleasured,
penetrated and finished,
almost but relieved of all its regal sins
in the bare, steamy desert
of human piles of dunes
and
sandy rolls of sweat.

I charcoaled the greenest eyes
and slathered gold through every inch
of my pale porcelain skin
wondering if I looked like her,
wanting to make you believe
that she still exists,
that she still belongs to you
through long nights of passion
and dreadful, sulking days,
for you,
my one and only,
for you,
my Mark Antony!

And I gloriously wait
inside the lace-covered tent
set up at the shaded oasis
by the ancient desert palms
where suitors are aplenty . . .
No need to overanalyze,
oh please, I beg you, my rebel Mark Antony,
your libido granted,
your stamina attested,
come closer, sweet lover.
The scorpions are waiting.
Like heroic legions they line up
to suck dry my Mark Antony . . .

Hurry up, my Mark,
your Cleopatra is losing patience.
Forget the toys and the servants,
the snakes are drooling
and we need their venom
to finish me first,
and then
go together!

So hurry back, sweet lover,
my lustful legionnaire,
for this Cleopatra needs her Mark Antony
like the wanton desert rose
back at the oasis . . .

The Silent Screaming Geisha

Each day starts the same:
the hot shower washes away
the amber scent of the night before,
the fresh makeup covers up
the forbidden radiance that only you know,
the impeccable flesh-covering dress,
the precise hair up in a bun,
the pearls and the open toe shoes
that perfectly match the plump red mouth.

While the day drifts away fast,
the night saves you the corner seat
to entertain with my silence,
to amuse with my existence.
As the red light goes up
and the curtain unfolds
and the world gets ready
around, I throw the gloves
but leave only your hat on . . .

With your perfect angelic smile
dressed in devil's seductive smirk—
ohm, you can never fool me,
you're not at all innocent!

I blame every January
and the first letter of the alphabet,
for that's where, when, and how
this eternal torment began.
I don't trust myself with you,
but I trust you will take care of me,
and trust is such an evil thing!
You have danced with me,
I have danced with you.
Were you meant for me?
Was I meant for you?
Maybe your God knows.
Mine's forgotten in Babylon.
Infected with your love,
tainted with your poison,
wrapped in your ever-changing alibi,
sealed with that longest January kiss . . .

I am indeed extraordinary
to your ordinary flame,
your strawberry Super Goddess
to your Eden's evergreen.
Quietly I rebel,
rebelliously I obey,
for I'm your silent screaming Geisha
praying that you'll want me again
every time you leave,
each time you come back!

KOZI NASI

Marry Me!

It needs to be pale pink,
the dress
that you will marry me in
someday,
not so jokingly, you say,
so you can see me blushing down the aisle
as the shy virgin that I was
when you first met me
last century.
Not so seriously, I agree.

On that rocky shore the altar shall be,
where the deep blue sea can envy you,
and the jealous waves can envy me,
and the purple horizon can testify
to the sleepless nights it's been spying on us
for decades now.

The stars shall be our happy witnesses.
The moon shall be the justice of peace
to bless our union with its illuminating shadow
as it shines down on our christening kiss!

You wish for me to bear one child with you—
a little girl, you say, as beautiful as me
so you and I live on in our little one,
so you can have me around old and young,
raise her as if you were raising me,
and if I am the first to pass on,
resembling me, through her you'll see . . .

So very little do you, crazy fool, know
that I was not made to fit
into a mortal's plan like this!

I was, in fact, born for you,
raised for you alone,
meant for you completely,
intended for you truly,
waited for you eagerly
to find me and keep me,
not to marry me,
not at all to make me a wife,
not to bear your offspring,
not to walk slowly down any aisles,
but purely, simply to belong to you
exactly the way you belong to me,
passionately,
lustfully,
cerebrally,
eternally!

Now
what do I say to you and your plan
when you look deep into my teary eyes,
lean down on a bended knee,
hold me by my trembling hands
and ask me
(with the eyes of the child
that badly wants his favorite toy),
"Will you marry me?"

Unconventional

A golden circle he gave me as a souvenir
to think of him by, as he was leaving me
to always remember the love that we shared,
the lust, the passion, the tears, the laughter.

Politely,
I gave it back before that last wet kiss,
reassuring him
the golden circle would do no good
to help me not forget,
asking him
to come find me whenever he returned,
promising
I'd forever see him
even if I were someday old and wrinkled,
even if I belonged to any another man—
I would see him no matter what,
like the forbidden secret lover
with whom you never really part . . .

Instead,
mad, mad lover swept me away
the wild unknown to uncover bare
with our virgin eyes and naked souls, he said.

Endless oceans and deep blue seas we crossed.
Forgotten were the vows of blood,
to have and to hold,
till death do us part,
for life and death are mine alone.

As I see you through your greatest adventure
with no prisons of tradition,
with no circles of gold,
with no *I do's* and *I don'ts,*
it's just you and I, lover,
the same endangered species
to the same wild unknown,
tied forever in circles of flesh,
sucking the gold out of this crazy life
then wearing it as teeth
to chew it slowly
bite
after
traditional bite!

KOZI NASI

The Story of a Long-Time Couple

I try not to ask you where or why,
but quietly,
I want to know it all.
You never ask me when or how many times,
but silently,
you read me like a book.

We do ask one another
every once in a while,
Anything new happened today?
and that is when our story begins
that is our sharing ritual.

I love you, not from a distance,
you love me, not from afar.
It's not so hard to cross that street; after all,
it all depends on who's waiting on the other side.

You know I'd leave the world for you.
I know you'd cheat them all for me.

We fight as if we're married.
We call each other names,
then make up as if we're strangers,
fornicate like rabbits,
happy just like clams, ah!

We don't need to cross that street after all.
No one is waiting on the other side.
You are
as good as it gets for me.
I am
your happy ending—
thus far!

Anniversary

I do! I do! I do!
Oh please, dear lover, ask me again
today,
in fifteen years to come,
and fifteen more after that.

I do! I do! I do!
Love the way you love me
just the way I am,
for no one else could.

I do! I do! I do!
Pray you let me love you
just the way you are,
the way I know how,
the only way I can.

For all of my weaknesses,
new wrinkles and dyed hair,
for all the quiet tears and the loud laughter,
for the fleeting mind and the ever-changing matter,
for all of your strengths,
your "always there" rock and your oh so tender care,
I hope we keep growing
by remaining the same!

On This Valentine's Day

I wish you had another woman tonight,
yet we both know deep down I'm not that generous
(no, I don't want to share you with any of them),
but I have a little plan, you see,
to still please you, I hope.

So,
for later, when we meet . . .
I shall straighten out my natural curls
and paint bloody red the lips,
black, fishnet thigh-high stockings
held with a garter on my hips,
and your favorite G-string
(for you to slip a dollar in!),
soft glitter on my porcelain skin
for you to find me in the dark
while I spin up and down the pole you've built in.

No, I will not be a French maid,
nor a genie in a bottle
to grant you every wish,
or some other lust-plumping fantasy—
as if you need any of it!

I shall be wonderland instead,
and let you climb gently, ride after ride,
from the tip of my toes
through the mile-long legs
to the top of your favorite hill, ah!
As you fight with the garter tattooed on my curves,
you rest but for a second
on that deep arched valley at the lowest of my back,
that one that for many years now
holds the secret to your magic.

I extend in pleasure
as you softly climb in
and toss me around through beaded and feathered pillows
as we limber in hysteria
of that moment of a pig, ah!
(I wish I were a pig!)

Where the neck meets the breasts,
right there is where you rest
and smell my ironed hair
and sniff my trembling skin
and sigh, happily relieved
that you've found me again!

I recognize that devilish twinkle in your brown suede eyes.
You lusted me different,
you liked the other woman,
the one that I gave you
just for tonight!

(PS: According to a study of *National Geographic Explorer,* a pig's orgasm lasts thirty minutes; don't we all wish we were pigs!)

Last Saturday Night

At the newest bar in town, you invite me to meet up,
and this Saturday night,
here, I wait
for you to come find me
like you always do,
in the farthest corner chair
in the poorest lit spot
wearing nothing but pearls
on your favorite long dress,
the one you've picked yourself
with the slit up the thigh
in the color of flesh . . .

Mindlessly
I chat with the young barkeeper
as he works to quench my thirst.
Anxiously
I run my fingers on the rim of my glass,
staring at my chipped red polish
left on purpose to come undone,
the naked shoulders facing the door,
the lighthouse atop the rocky shore
to your tired ship on its way home.
But you are
unusually late . . .

A stranger offers me companionship
as a true gentleman,
and sweetly slips me his phone number
folded into a happy origami.
He sticks it in my curls
while helping me pick up the pearls
that broke free from the string choking my neck.
I find him handsome,
and kind as well.
To thank him, I throw my generous smile
as if to hide the sadness inside.
I feel him melt deep into my eyes,
so to please him I promise I shall call,
but promises are meant to be broken—
little does he know . . .

The last one's on me, the young barkeeper offers
at closing time—he and I remain alone.
The lights are all dimmed,
chairs all up on the tables,
some faraway tune lingers painfully around . . .

He calls me beautiful while filling my glass
as I get up to dance
the slow,
sad,
mellow tune
that's got me wondering what happened to you,
that's got me wondering what's happening with me
on a Saturday night like this
with inviting faces
and broken promises . . .

I find myself alone in my cold, big bed,
one side made up,
my side a mess.
In no hurry to know, I slowly touch myself.
The dress is still on, but no shoes and no pearls.
Two origami sit quietly on my nightstand.
A deep sigh of relief exhales from my chest!
What a night, I whisper, holding my head,
in my parched mouth,
the taste of a wet dream,
everywhere else,
the friendliest pain!

(Lover did come find me—
he just happened to be
late,
unusually!)

Still

Deep in thought, you sit at the end of the plush couch,
in one hand,
some Bordeaux in a crystal glass,
the other
playing with my toes on your lap.
We've just finished
making love,
and sex after that.
We used to cuddle around this time years ago.
Now we sit and talk like two great friends.
I must confess,
this part, now, I enjoy even more.

Yet tonight, you're unusually silent
as if you're trying to decide in your head,
not whether or not tell me,
but rather wondering if you should ask.

You forget, sweet lover,
that ever since we met
you were always the quiet one
(a birth defect, I called it then).
I've trained myself to read you, since,
by the corners of your eyes, how they focus and cringe,
by the edge of your mouth, how it holds the tongue inside,
by your forehead, how it wrinkles in that single line,
by your chin, how it comes up,
by your ears, how they both go back at once,
by your temples, how they pulsate,
and that famous mole at the lower lip
that so many times gently I've rested my fingers
to stop you from going on . . .

But tonight, you're awfully quiet,
and me, too lazy to read you,
and for a minute it does feel
like the other shoe, any second will drop!
When you suddenly let go of my toes
to rest your glass, bend over on the table,
pull my legs abruptly around your waist,
grab me and sit me on your lap,
stroking gently my red messy curls,
look me deep in the eye,
and whisper as you sigh:
kiss me,
kiss me,
then again kiss me some!

I hate it when you change your mind
and realize that your wisdom has talked you out
of asking me what you really need to find,
the very thing I confirmed just now:
yes, I still do!
and deep down,
I wish you still do too!

Your head rests comfortably on my sleepy chest.
The dim moonlight sneaks through the blinds
softly shining on the squeezed strawberries
leftover, forgotten, on the nightstand to your right . . .

Good Night!

The darkness swallowed my soft *good night*
hesitantly . . .
I surrendered you to your sleep of death,
the only kind
your tiredness needs for now.

With your head on my chest, you close your eyes,
the world's softest pillow,
yours for the night.
I find myself counting burnt lashes,
rubbing your deep lines,
impure as the fantasy
that lingers between your temples . . .

But you are tired indeed,
and your failing attempt to stay with me longer,
it's sadly romantic,
and as such I won't have it!

Forget about your troubles
and the dramas that caused them,
forget the illusive dreams
and the flesh that surrounds them,
forget to wake up
from your lively, cozy pillow,
forget everything!
Till you can no longer recall
the generous soul
that lullabied you happy
to your lazy, empty sleep
with that softest *good night*
in the world's softest pillow
that you gladly borrowed
and I happily offered
one
last
time . . .

Break

Not liking the beach today.
In fact, I must have a break
from the sun and the beach.
I did enjoy it very much yesterday,
yet it tired me in the end.
Today I rest
and recuperate
and distill my thoughts
and try to figure a different kind of life.
So I write.
I write about my feelings,
my troublesome worries,
my dead inspirations,
my uninspiring heroes.
I write about the unsung melodies in my lips
waiting to be danced between my feet . . .

So I write:
the cheapest therapy
for an expensive girl like me!

Lazy

Lazy,
to want to bother with the world—
it best come get me!
Lazy,
to want to move—
they best push me off this old bed!
Lazy,
to get out of my borrowed blue boxers—
lover best undress me!
Lazy,
to stretch my arms and legs—
he best massage me!
Lazy,
to sip my nose tickling, liquid adrenaline—
he best pour it in me!
Lazy,
to even open my mouth—
he best come kiss it!

Never, ever, ever, lazy,
to throw around my grateful, happy smile,
for such infinite contentment,
for such softest,
most gentle,
the sweetest awake!

On a Given Sunday

Oh, how regrettable,
to leave things as they were last night
and opt for sleep.
Now I wake up obligated to attend.
We must all suffer some kind of punishment
for every drop of fun we have.

Yes, last night was fun:
the faces,
the wine,
the conversations,
the more wine, again,
the sleep on the way back,
lover's magic hands,
the long drive as well,
the fun hangover of the late twenties,
the staying headache of the late thirties,
the "easy to collapse on" couch nearby,
the "must undress for" bed afar,
the clothes on, then off,
the blanket,
the waiting,
the decision to drag my ass to bed,
the oh so soft pillow,
the oh so big and comfy bed,
the moment,
the joy,
that joy, ah!
the pass out!

And now,
I reach for the black coffee
with two sugars,
one milk,
and do not wish to look at the clothes on the floor . . .

While some music in the background sings,
Up, up and away!
I silently beg, *No, not today!*

But I must,
and here I am,
thinking out loud,
I wish I had a butler and a maid!
Hey, it's my dream!

While reality laughs in my face
and offers me more coffee
with a soft, gentle massage
for my late thirties' unkind pain . . .

Inside My Head

Self-inflicted aneurysm—
the head boils and the blood splatters
and the spirit of what I used to be
evaporated
a few playful moons ago—
my head is no place for pure blood—
impurely
I must suck it all dry
and deliver me to the next affliction
that stubbornly has me reserved
for life!

Dilemma

Reality and Dreamland
are at each other's throats
for my attention today.
I lay neutral and just wait.
I know that I'm the only one
who can put an end to this.
To drag it out for a little while longer
for now is all I want!
Slowly, I separate the upper lashes
tangled with the bottom ones,
only to catch the sky graying my window—
yet another morning.

I root for Dreamland,
but Reality
has a leg up on this one,
definitely!

So, unwillingly I choose,
and begin to stretch
and shake away the night's folds.
Off I go,
Onward and upward! I say to Reality
See you when the night falls, I whisper to Dreamland.

Not a Long Note

You ask me to write you something long,
and believe me, I really want to as well,
but I am not ready for a love letter!

You ask me to give you my lips,
and passionately I want to lose mine in yours,
but I am not ready for the bloodiest kiss!

You ask me to stay when next to you naked I lie,
and ever so happily I wish to comply,
but I am not ready to be the remarrying type!

You tell me you love me the more that you know me,
and gently I whisper in the back of your ear,
but I am not ready to stop having fun!

Instead,
I kiss the tired corners of your quietly melting eyes,
I free fall in your embrace as if it were my final resting place,
I slide under your skin and flow freely in your veins,
I rejuvenate your blood with my impure oxygen,
I sing you to sleep and wake you up with a new melody,
I surrender myself to you in endless hours of lustful love,
I miss you and crave you when we are apart,
I pray that this story lasts forever and ever
so I can come to get buried in your burning flame
when I deliver you my incandescent soul
like the lines on this note I write you tonight
in the *you*-shaped bed,
watching the sun rise . . .

Relax

You're near and far at once,
and I can't go on without you or with you.
I need to be able to find your eyes in the dark
so through the sunrise they can guide my dreams
and scare away in hiding the nightmares!
It's not simply black and white.
Relax;
it's paradoxical monochromatic instead,
my Max!

The desert to your oasis, I drink you like the thirsty canary,
yet every drop leaves me more parched for you.
Amidst golden feathers, your temptress lover, I float
above your tumultuous, troubled waters until I
relax,
on your left shoulder, right above your heart, I rest,
my Max!

This is a glorious morning's dream, in fact,
pink as my blushing, usually pale cheeks
when you gaze at me on the way out
the door that releases you into
the eagerly expecting world
that you happily give yourself to,
relaxed,
that you and I,
near or far,
with or without,
will soon meet again,
my Max!

Later, Please!

I am out of my mind,
and I know your fears
like you know my pain,
and I can't sleep tonight,
am terrified of the dreams
that might come visit.

Unhealthy
is my state of mind.
Feel free to judge, love;
tonight I do not care.
Paint me all over
with the heavy brush
of your traitorous conscience.
Let me be
the plain canvas
of that blank picture frame
we bought on that exotic trip
but never bothered to hang.

Do what you wish
with me tonight.
I am here for you,
but out of my mind.

Say what you think,
hear what you care;
I can only exist
as a mute and a blind.

KOZI NASI

Turn me upside down,
then downside up again.
Undress me at first,
but don't bother to dress me back.
I am out of my mind
and in no mood to care.

We'll talk in the morning
when the rain has disappeared.
Tomorrow, we'll continue this
when I can gladly use
my semi-rested cerebellum.

Later, I beg you,
later,
please,
oh, please!

Vincent

Van Gogh knocked on my door tonight.
He said he wanted to have just dinner
and talk, to catch up.
Neither suited me,
yet happily I complied.

Van Gogh took me out tonight;
to borrow my soul for his pillow he begged
and *Promise to bring it in the morning,*
in the thickest accent he said.
Hesitantly, again I complied
(wondering if without it
I could ever survive).

Van Gogh dropped me off tonight.
It was a fun evening, just the two of us,
and for old time's sake
he even kissed me at my door,
excusing himself for having cut it short,
yet hours and hours had gone by.
(I never bothered questioning that man.
I loved him too much,
and he always had a reason why!)

Vincent called me to step out
in the wee hours of the morning.
Trembling and shaking, he gave me a gift
while hating himself for his generosity.
He gave me the burning kiss,
that famous one
he always gave when he would leave,
and whispered in my ear
things I wasn't supposed to hear.
Rest assured,
I madly, deeply love you, my dear,
adore you, need you,
ever so near
to touch you and hold you
as if you weren't real,
for then I could breathe
at the comfort of your inexistence.
So accept this gift from me
for you, with all my heart.
I did borrow your soul,
but you should keep my blood—
use it if you must,
swallow it drop by drop,
but only to nurture
your marvelous affection
you so generously throw around!

He ran away with the dawn,
no farewell,
no good-bye . . .

Frozen, there I stood,
not knowing what to make of it.
With me: the bleeding ear
coagulating faster
than his disappearance.

He could live on my soul,
but not I
in his tainted dead blood!
You hear me, Vincent?
You could never love me much too much!
My soul shall remind you of such.
It will always remind you
for the rest of your life!

Toxic

The glasses weigh down on my half-blind eyes,
tiring my nose as they tilt to the left.
My head feels numb on the warm, bare shoulders.
It suffocates, surrounded by melodramatic thoughts in vain
that bite little pieces of my abused cerebellum.

The glasses fog up,
much like my damp thoughts,
from the clouds of the evaporating silent tears
that quietly descend off the two olive trees
that shade the irises of my aching soul.

And you,
you're not here to watch me unload,
so in that sinful moment's heat
to release and set free
my piled-on longing with my filed-away dreams.

I should have let you come over, you know.
I should have let you beg, like only you never do.
I should have you here, now,
to be my magic oyster and shorten this damn long night,
undress me of my steamed-up glasses,
untangle my hurting thoughts one by one,
stretch out smooth my pleated cerebellum wrinkles,
push me to drown into oblivion,
help me drift off under your skin
where deeply I hide, happily delusional,
and deliriously inhale
this heavily contaminated,
toxically flavored,
last, new life!

Giving Up!

Tonight I've decided:
I shall take a break
from my art and my artists!

I shall leave them all for a minute,
no Mona Lisa for my Leonardo,
no Elise for my Ludwig,
no Nun for my Diderot.

I shall give up my painters, sculptors, and musicians—
to Hell with the whole Louvre—
to Hell with it
just for a little while!

Tonight I prefer a long, warm bath
to rid me of my filth in the deepest Niagara
and seduce God instead.
He seems to be the most capable suitor
to keep up with this game.

Yet tonight, I write alone
alongside quiet Seine, in the City of Love.
No stars, just the wind is my only friend
as it wraps itself around me
like the arms I so badly long for
as it caresses my left ear,
accidentally brushing my left breast,
much like the strange tongues

I yearn and yearn to hear
and decipher nonetheless.
Butterflies all tangled inside,
the wind throws them off for a loop.
The City of Love has gotten them drunk.
The City of Love has turned off its lights!

Tonight I give up
on all my humanly art
and invite God to my deepest Niagara bath of sins
and beg him to (one by one) dip his toes
in the foaming, troubled waters
and splash me to the rebirth
of his divine christening!
Laughing hysterically,
I shall give him a burning kiss
with the softest inside of my lips
as the tongue happily dances behind my teeth.
Wash me—I shall let him
dry me as well, ah!
And dress me in his sin-free spell,
for tonight, I take a break.
Tonight, I'm giving up
just for a very short,
little
while!

The Last Sweet Adventure

It's been awhile now,
and it's been together, lover,
every each morning,
every each night,
every each day.
The room suffocates with the two of us in it,
desperate to fill up when one of us is away.

It's been a good while, love.
Have we known each other this long,
or did time get tired of us?
We talk through impatient breaths
in tongues only birds can decipher,
yet the flesh remains the same,
trembling within
the everlasting desire . . .

I do not wish to take.
I do not think to abuse.
I could not have you.
I can only but leave you.
So I take my melting ice cubes
from my favorite whiskey glass.
Diluted, I conclude, as I can no longer swallow.
Time to start fresh,
accidentally you utter.

In the middle of the desert,
I shall plant my offering tree
with my greenest olive eyes
as the perfect fertile seed.
I shall water it with my tears,
the quiet, salty ones you left behind.
I shall wait till it grows tall and strong,
strong as you and I were once.
With its long, peaceful branches
I shall softly caress
from a vibrant, blurry distance
your elongating shadow
as you slowly drift away
on the reddish-purple sunset,
while I, lungs full, breathe in
the last sweet adventure!

The Wind and I

Two anniversaries have the wind and I,
one every first snow,
the other every first flower,
and the rest of the year we simply go back
from December to April to December again.

It has yet to snow this year, my wind,
am all ears on the crazy weather man.
When it does,
together we shall drink
up there, where the clouds are thick,
not champagne, but a half o' century old bottle of rain
we've left hidden from the last time,
and we shall smoke as well,
pieces of our very own pheromone sky
that you happily sniff as it evaporates from my skin,
and then finally we shall kiss,
not the tongue slithering so-called French,
but fearlessly throat deep,
while sky-floating real high.

My head on your feathery shoulder I shall rest when done,
holding on for dearest death whilst you fly me away
atop gray craters of patient volcanos
where lazy lava for the spark to erupt awaits,
as we birth our very own immaculate dream,
my wind and I,
me and my wind.

The waves will get jealous
when at the ocean to quench our thirst we'll stop
and I'll listen to you enthrall me with your tales of exhausted
passion.
Stuck, entangled, we remain in each other's doomed love,
only to meet twice a calendar,
some newly unknown place afar
where purposefully we mistake canaries for doves . . .

Two anniversaries have the wind and I,
one every first snow,
the other, every first flower,
and the rest of the year we simply go back
from December to April to December again.

No little white flurries yet,
says the crazy weather man!

If Only!

I don't know what to do with you,
my most familial of strangers,
my uninvited little slight,
my friendliest of pains,
my filthiest of habits,
my strongest of addictions,
my sandiest of deserts,
my windiest of hurricanes,
my wettest of tropics,
my hottest of equators,
my coldest of Antarctics,
my deepest of icebergs,
my tallest of Everests,
my splashiest of waterfalls,
my roughest of seas,
my shortest of nights,
my Aprilest of springs,
my loudest of drums,
my gentlest of guitars,
my airiest of touches,
my longest of embraces,
my bloodiest of kisses,
my lustiest of desires,
my heartiest of laughters,
my weariest of longings,
my dearest of sadnesses,
my vividest of dreams,
my most impossible possible,
ah!

If only you were
my truest of loves!

KOZI NASI

While You Were Gone

While you were gone,
the longest month turned into the shortest one.
In the strangely warm coldest season,
a few winter birds tangled their feathers
and gave life to new snuggling tweets.
Time moved on as it always did.
Seconds became minutes,
minutes became hours,
until I forgot to count.
The sun rose with every dawn
and went down every time the moon asked nicely.
No flowers bloomed by accident,
and the naked trees continued to breathe bare.
The waterfalls gracefully obeyed gravity,
happily splashing rainbows on their liquid way down.
Sixty-nine shooting stars gave birth to a brand-new wish—
everything went about its life,

but I . . .

I didn't shed a precious tear,
yet didn't have the heart to sing,
tried hard to find solace
in the colorless cloak of a monk,
and gave up on the struggle
to remember how you sound.
You bragged I could never forget you
but forgot to remember that Time
is nothing but a cruel magician
in a "killing me softly" invisible disguise!

While you were gone,
I sat on your favorite chair,
thought of you fondly,
and wrote down these lines . . .

Against This One Bird!

I do not like the metal bird up above.
I do not wish to hear its name.
It took the sun away from me.
All I have left are clouds,
gray clouds aplenty dirtying my sky . . .

I hate the metal bird up above.
I shall not speak its ugly name.
It took lover away.
All I have left is sad space,
waterless, drowning, empty space surrounding me—
tick-tock, tick-tock, tick-tock.

A red-striped shirt is what I like for now,
and the zippered sweater I found on the floor
and some black socks.
The red stripes of the shirt,
the zipper of the sweater,
and the soft socks are glued to my skin.
They have promised to keep it warm for now . . .
Take that you, cold metal bird!

Without a Muse.

My muse has left me high and dry.
(No one else will do!)
I couldn't return the love in time.
All around me, a silent gray shadow lingers ...

Crazy, stubborn muse,
what do you know of me?

Above the Clouds

I was up there.
I sat higher than the plush clouds,
swallowed the salt of my quiet tears . . .
I talked to the biggest orange sun I found in that winter sky,
begged it to send you my trembling warmth
to make you feel my love . . .

Hiding

I left.
I ran
far, far away
where no clouds could cover me
and the heavy feathered birds
got tired of entertaining me . . .

And I've lost all right of return,
for this prodigal child
can never go back!

Dove Mail

I shed only one single heavy tear
before I turned myself into a bird.
I sent it to you
with the first white dove I found, on my way to conversion,
for you to drink it in tiny drops
and quench your screaming thirst for me
while I'm gone . . .

Ether

(the other woman)

Swallowed I am by ether,
pathetic old ether is choking me.
I do not love ether,
but for her to feel alive,
ether needs me.

I run for the match to flame it all up.
I'm on the eighth of this cat's nine lives.
Generous I must be with ether, though,
and graciously give that very last ninth.

Take it, ether;
take it you sad, evaporating soul,
and next time you see me,
don't come to say hi!
Don't look me in the eye,
or thank me at all.
Do me a huge favor
and don't try to survive.
I can only be kind
this once in your lifetime.
The grass is definitely greener
on my other side!

One's Love of Their Life.

You can take all the body parts
and frame them as a souvenir
or a lucky sixty-nine,
then
dive head first
into your warm pool of filthy, inviting sin.
You are still stuck with her in mind
and no time or whores aplenty
could cure your disease
so
you quietly let her be,
like the constant, friendly headache
I can live without . . .

Sticky bodies come and go
to help you feed your taunted monkey.
The stench of fornication is there to remind you
of the sleeping giant
that's got you hooked like a junkie!
It is the longing for her I see
in all your failed conquests,
mixed in with your incapacitated will
to want to let her go,
much like
the favorite strawberry-flavored semen I prefer
after all the sushi dinners
I can't live without!

Go ahead, dearest;
don't give it another thought.

Don't give it more time.
You have but the souvenir
to help you reminisce
on her
and your lucky sixty-nine!

This Fall's Dead Leaves.

What a performance!
I expected the curtain to come down on me.
I got the fall instead
(my favorite season, I'll admit),
and this fall's fainting leaves.

Scattered,
my thoughts wander in the dry desert
on their way to the warm, inviting migration, mindlessly.
The scavenger bird spread them around carelessly
while it feasted on my poisoned flesh,
not forgetting to lick all two hundred and eight bones
of my fragile skeleton.

Scared,
the vulture bird flew away.
Eviscerated,
my carcass consoles my orphan thoughts.
My mind is numb, can't feel the pain.
The carnivore bird kept for himself
the deepest seventh layer of my skin.
Now the upper six have nowhere to stick.
Exposed, I feel,
and my flesh is unwrapped
and I bleed
my rare purple blood for you, I bleed.
Dipped in it,
this fall's dying leaves . . .

I despise this hellish game
where you find me and lose me
and after bedding the devil, come look for me again.
Ever the torturous sadist, I crave my pain,
with you, the mad masochist
who loves to hurt me just the same.

I bleed, and no thirsty travelers care to drink me.
They can tell
I'm poisoned to death with your spell.
What have I done?
What did you give me?
Why did you throw me
this fall's dead leaves?
Breathe life back in me, oh you, fall's sweetest leaves,
the life that escapes you every third season,
and in the fourth, can't wait to start in me!
Bring me to life, you stubborn fall's leaves.
In return, I promise to keep you forever
and silently convert you
into my last secret lover
in my dying hour of need!

Dearest criminal stranger,
am I being punished for not finding you sooner,
or are you too late to have just found me?

The right side belongs to the sun,
the left to the lightning,
and me in the middle
of colorless, lifeless piles
of this fall's dead leaves . . .

KOZI NASI

Sacrifice

Don't come looking for me, you angel of death,
or better yet,
come, if you'd please,
even though
I still have a few precious minutes left
out of the eleven months I've already spent
from the year I borrowed to deliver myself.

I have made up my mind, I promise.
You take me and set him free.
I will smile, I will look pretty,
I shall dance, I shall sing!

I have made up my mind to run and fly
five thousand stubborn miles away.
I shall only leave behind
my porcelain skin and the flowers of blood
and the golden leaves I used for pins
and the pale lips,
forgotten, bitten on the right side,
and the empty dead eyes . . .

There's this pressure in my head
to try and keep up with you.
Under pressure I do not fare well.

So come and get me, you angel of death,
before I change my mind,
before the loud echoing "I do!"
me and lover exchange for good
there, at the edge of life!

Russian Roulette

Loud
was the sound of the gunshot.
It rang even louder
next to my right ear,
deafening the world around me,
disappearing in the sonar cloud.
Cold
felt the gray metal on my right temple
as he took all the pleasure in the world,
pressing at it every single time,
tormenting me with his favorite game
of Russian roulette.
Every time a bullet skipped,
fate loved me another round . . .

I knew it'd soon be my turn—
unlucky for him, for generous I was not.
I never had a flair for weak, pathetic games.
Grimly leaning on my steady feet,
inhaling deep the last trembling breath,
point blank I aimed,
stared him long in his dead eyes,
freeing my soul from the captive fear.
Oh so gently, I pulled that anxious trigger,
releasing my pain with the eager bullet!
Happily, I left the residue on,
but wiped off the smirk on the way out
(conscience footed my freedom's toll).

The bloody ending spilled on the sunset,
red painting the next thirsty beginning.
Nourished I remain today.
The right temple still hates
every crisp thunder!

Cemeteries

It is a habit of mine to walk through cemeteries
where old spirits come to party
for lack of being able to die.

In a mood like my habit I walk tonight:
tombstones—the invited gentlemen,
decorative statues—the entertaining whores,
marbled photographs—the fake IDs
for the ageless souls of the decaying skeletons.

Myself to entertain amidst ghosts I wish tonight,
so I brought my whitest sheet
with the bubbliest champagne supernova,
sparkly like the brightest June star
that shamelessly bribes the jealous moon
to brighten up my ethereal path,
where I watch myself transform
into tiny pieces of galactic twinkles.

It is here
my uninterrupted solitude begins
and haunting memories of past loves
and faces
and bodies
and voices
and echoes
and melodies
and symphonies
clutter my soul to despair . . .

It is here
my poetically rejuvenated, subdued mellow
feels seductively ADD,
while I dive in the largest ghostly orgy
right here, in the purest, whitest sheet
I brought together with the bottle o' bubbly.

My flesh disintegrates
only to dress the skeletons
that eagerly wish to join in and reminisce
(much like me)
on the bygone days where love was traded free
from body to body and spirit to spirit!

The spirits have gotten me cerebrally euphoric
(one in particular).
Undressed of my flesh, I roam the cemetery,
free to visit wherever I please,
with the wings of a new love
that spins my world around,
so I get to relive my thousandth life
from death number 999!

It is a habit of mine
to walk through cemeteries
where blood has no color or coagulation time,
yet it flows steadily through my tangled arteries
wrapped on all seven layers of my transparent skin
on my skeleton body
in complete piece with all my sins
in utter repentance
with all my loves,
all but one,
this very last one!

Immortal

Don't know if I prefer death
for the sake of a beautiful funeral
where crocodiles come to claim their tears,
or a lonely cremation for the sake of love,
where I get to come back on my cat's ninth life.

I sure hope to burn
and burn and burn and burn,
until my naked skeleton is freed
of all my fleshly sins—
they can judge that all they want!

And I shall not ask you to join me,
'cause in the end, love,
we all go alone
when our own borrowed time is up!

(But the sinners remain undead
with immortality
as their eternal punishment!)

Non-cooperating Buddha!

The converted Buddha is awfully quiet.
That's what I get for my incapacitated will
to bother inquiring . . .

It was I who spoiled him
with delicious fumes
of mind erasing Heavenly liquids,
for all pleasures have their own price!

Look at me, Buddha,
you old friend of mine,
come cheer me up,
happy me just a little
or a lot,
if you must.

I'll attend to the liquid,
you, to the night
and while we're at it,
let's rip it,
let's tear it apart
and give it as a black tissue
for dawn's gray clouds . . .

It will be a long night, Buddha.
If you've decided to keep this up,
forget meditation.
(We'll get back to that in the morning.)
This little party of two
is only for tonight.

Say something, damn it,
open your mouth
or do something,
or forget it
or forget me
(not)!

Forgotten Winter in the Land of Cedar

The wind screeches loudly on the cold outside,
fiercely wanting to push itself in.
A happy fire burns slowly on the old brick fireplace,
generously caressing with long tongues of flames
two logs burning
in their last blazing hug.

The tired teakettle invitingly whistles loud.
The fringed green blanket at the feet of the couch
quietly enjoys a solemn break
from being used to warm
the heavy-breathing bodies and the kisses on the floor.
An oversized plaid scarf still thrown without a purpose,
the crackle of the logs at war with the whistling kettle,
a faraway mellow tune stuck on replay,
a silent guitar is dreaming to be touched
by the fireplace where the red bra calls for its breasts.
Gray is the sky
and the first lost snowflake
just wandered on by
for the very first time
on my thirty-eighth January
in my land of Cedar . . .

Therapy

This big empty bag I grabbed a long time ago
and stuffed it with all advice I was ever given.
I shoved it all in there,
the good mixed with the bad,
the idiotic with the wise,
the conservative with the daring,
the inspirational with the ignorant,
the encouraging with the critical,
the fake with the polite,
the heartfelt with the hypocritical,
the cautious with the strict,
the hands off-ish with the supportive,
the pure with the insulting,
the remarkable with the cheap—
what a tricky bag it turned out to be!

I let it breathe from time to time
and air it out piece by piece
before I squeeze it all back in . . .

The precious bag never leaves my sight.
While the well of secrets trembles and shrieks,
it fearfully hesitates to spill.
Abused by the advice and the good will,
yet sadistically stubborn, it pushes me
to flood the world with the secret waters deep . . .

Let's make up our minds, the three of us,
the well of secrets,
me,
and my bag of advice,
which, for the advisers' sake, I shall call it here on out
my bag of strait-jacket therapy!

The Year of the Rabbit

It was the Year of the Rabbit in the Chinese calendar.
It was the Year of the Chaos in mine,
as stories of all sorts came and went
and places with faces
and lovers as well.

A mad year it was,
when just like that, halfway through,
a beautiful stranger from worlds away
decided to appear in my universe of blue.

I knew I had dreamt him
through my far-gone teenage years
when I longed for that caped magician
who would help me disappear . . .
and now in my old age,
answered are my prayers!

Softly he spoke when in a happy mood,
so happy I made him to taste his softness.
Gently, he touched every inch of my skin
so I let him touch it whenever he wanted.
Flowers he would plant on my lips with every kiss
so ready to bloom, every night for him I waited . . .

KOZI NASI

Naturally, in my Chaotic Year of the Rabbit,
I was being pulled and pushed
again and again,
broken to pieces that could never be glued back,
tossed and turned and sniffed and breathed,
lusted after and made love to, oh so endlessly . . .
Then it happened, on a surreally calm day.
We were sitting close,
flesh and skin a-holding,
when he said he wanted me to be his last station,
the very last one where he had come to stay
and spend with me his remaining days . . .
I sat quietly as boiling tears showered my face.
The gray hair of old age lost the artificial red.
The thought of belonging I had craved for so many years
finally here, as life was passing in a flash.
In the shivering palms of my hands I carried his face
and covered it with the warmest kisses I could ever give
from my bleeding soul, not from my lips,
staring him deep in his warm, good eyes.
I shook my head and blinked
to promise him such:
that I would love him as greatly as only I knew how,
always passionately,
with every beat of my heart!

No need for stations or conductors alike,
he could come and go as he pleased.
I would wait by the fireplace night after night,
enflamed with my Chaos,
engulfed with my Love,
in that Year of the Rabbit
of the Chinese calendar.

A Fairy Tale for a Lady in the Making

She takes me by her little hand
with her sparkly, twinkling eyes,
begs me for a fairy tale
Oh, but please, a very short one!
Weakened by her plea,
I think but for a moment
until slowly I begin . . .

Three fairies got together.
Waving away their glittery wands,
off to sleep they put the little one
to wake her up in thirty-seven years of life.

A prince they sent in the meantime
who bestowed upon her a feathery kiss,
then a glass slipper slid on her foot
and in a two-horse carriage
flew her to the moon.

There they set up house for a good long time,
not bothered by weightlessness or lack of oxygen.
A love nest they built
on earth's only satellite,
and happily ever after,
they lived amongst the stars—
he, the handsome prince,
she, the fairy-wand-hypnotized bride.

As year thirty-seven approached nearer and nearer,
the little one and her prince awaited with fear,
wondering if the wearing-off of the fairy spell
would crumble away their cozy love nest.

Little did they know,
those two crazy lovebirds,
that up there in the moon,
space cannot be measured and all time is erased,
so year thirty-seven came and went!

Thus, forever they lived, loving one another,
thinking any moment could be their very last,
humbly grateful to the three lady fairies
for their wand-waving spell
and their magical dust!

But in life, unlike fairy tales,
there's no such happily ever after.
You can't wait for love, hypnotized under
if you look for it, you find it;
if you find it, you keep it;
if you keep it, you love it
and cherish it eternally!

And my sweet little angel closes her eyes,
drifts off to sleep,
beginning to dream
her own fairy tale of love,
nighty-night,
nighty-night!

KOZI NASI